Mrs A. Varner -
No 13

FLOWER ARRANGEMENTS

FLOWER ARRANGEMENTS

EXAMPLES OF THE AUTHOR'S ARRANGEMENTS
OF FLOWERS AND FOLIAGE OF HAWAII AND
OTHER PARTS OF THE UNITED STATES

BY CAROLINE E. PETERSON

AN AMERICAN STUDIO BOOK

THE STUDIO PUBLICATIONS, INC. · NEW YORK & LONDON

DEDICATION

To Kauai—land of my birth.
"Resplendent island,
  A pearl for the race,
  Permeated with the sweetness
  And the fragrance of Hawaii,
  And the eight Seas."

CONTENTS

ACKNOWLEDGMENTS

I wish to thank my many friends in the Islands and throughout the American continent for their spontaneous interest in my work.

I am deeply grateful for the opportunity of being associated with the Honolulu Academy of Arts, for it is in such beautiful surroundings that inspiration flourishes and may be expressed.

Special thanks are due Mrs. Theodore A. Cooke, Mrs. Philip E. Spalding, Mrs. George P. Cooke, Mr. Robert Allerton, Mrs. Richard A. Cooke, Mrs. Alice Spalding Bowen, Mrs. Atherton Richards, Mrs. Walter F. Dillingham, and Mr. C. C. Bailey, whose interest, assistance, and belief in my work have inspired me to produce a book of my arrangements.

My aloha and heartfelt thanks go to Mrs. Catharine E. B. Cox; my daughter, Muriel, and her husband, Lt. General Edwin W. Rawlings; to my youngest son, Robert, and his business partner, Mr. Donald Woodrum, Jr.; and to all the members of my family for their encouragement of my project and their many hours of thought and effort in helping me prepare my book for publication.

FOREWORD

A MESSAGE

In Hawaii . . . in other parts of the United States . . . in almost every garden or countryside . . . there are blossoms, leaves, branches, pods, et-cetera, which may be seen but not always remembered as possible materials for decorating. My search for new materials, or for novel uses for commonplace materials, is never-ending; it seems to go on almost subconsciously wherever I happen to be.

Plants and fruits and sheaths . . . coral and wood and tin . . . all are excellent possibilities. Even the lowly cabbage acquires a lively personality if used with imagination and a little practice. Therefore, it is my wish that this book will stimulate others to be ever watchful for materials which, with imagination, can be arranged into pleasant and striking pieces for the home. I know of no limit to things which can be used—and certainly there is no end of ideas envisioned by an active imagination—so, I hope this book will bring pleasure to those who read it and study the illustrations. Each arrangement was an adventure . . . in each there was anticipation and hard work and satisfaction . . . and in each some expression of my fondness for flowers and plants.

Caroline E. Peterson.

7

INTRODUCTION

This book illustrates the original, creative work of Mrs. Caroline E. Peterson in flower arrangement. It does not attempt to develop theories or rules, for, as Mrs. Peterson herself declares, she does not work from formal rules. Nevertheless, the elements of good design and interesting composition are apparent in all her work—the work of a truly gifted artist.

The illustrations are a selection of arrangements made for special occasions and places. Even apart from their settings, which frequently enhanced their beauty, they indicate the wide range of her styles, her fertile imagination and her natural sensitiveness, played upon by many stimulating influences in Hawaii and other parts of the United States.

Mrs. Peterson, born in the Islands, inherited that joyous responsiveness to Nature that gave rise to the traditional Hawaiian religions and social observances—that still linger in the charming use of the symbolic "lei" (garland), the fern and leaf-bedecked settings for "luaus" (feasts) and the dress of hula dancers.

The "leis" and wreaths of Hawaii are as characteristic and meaningful as the Greek garlands.

The lavish productiveness of the tropical growth where flowering trees, shrubs and brightly colored leaves make these Islands a riot of color and fragrance, give rise to a fascinating exhuberance and stimulation to create bold combinations in line, in texture, and in masses of color. With a natural gift of responsiveness to rhythm and dramatic effects, Mrs. Peterson has been quick to realize the possibilities of Oriental line arrangements and of modern, stylized simplicity and audacity. She uses all sorts of material in her arrangements—bare branches of trees, stems of plants, the dull rich color and odd shapes of vegetables, rocks, coral and shells—in fact, almost everything that springs from Nature.

Mrs. Peterson must find expression as she does —in arranging the elegant and the graceful— and even the humorous and the whimsical—for her Muse of Beauty has been inspiring her these many years of her artistry with flowers.

CATHARINE E. B. COX

Honolulu, T. H.

1948

COLOR

TROPICAL REDS

The solidity and formal arrangement of rich, opaque colors—the dark red bananas and their maroon-stained leaves—contrast with the gay enchantment of the capricious red orchid. The flat bowl is crystal, the table mahogany, and the whole arrangement a striking dinner decoration.

TOOLS AND IMPLEMENTS

The following equipment was used for the arrangements throughout the book.

ANCHORING AND PINNING

Spiked holder   *Greening pins*

Papaya (substitutions are cabbage, banana plant section, squash)

CUTTING AND SLICING

Heavy scissors   *Trimming clippers*   *Knife*   *Vegetable slicer*

BINDING AND TYING

22 or 24 gauge copper wire   *Ti leaves (substitutions are aspidistra leaves or raffia)*

Pandanus (a substitution is Iris leaves — dry or green).

Photo: Werner Stoy

Photo: Werner Stoy

ORIGINAL CONTAINERS

The fruit basket (left) and flower basket (right) have been fashioned from young coconut fronds. The white lines of the coconut leaves cover a gallon can, and the fruit basket is made of these same coconut leaf sections woven into a mat with loose, extended ends tied into four knots. The Egyptian Papyrus is anchored on a spiked holder which has been hidden from view by a fence of papyrus stems. Other material in the different parts of the country could be utilized, as, for example, the Pandanus in Florida. Iris leaves, dry or green, can be woven into an original basket and arranged in a pleasing decoration that has personality and beauty.

12

FANTASY

Day lilies of tawny, coppery tones . . . green branches of Cotoneaster . . . and leaves fashioned from sheet copper are the materials which went into this fanciful arrangement. The leaves, curled and reeded into dramatic lines, were shaped with an ordinary little metal-working tool found in art stores. Also fashioned from sheet copper were the container, to conceal the spiked holder, and the tray with rolled ends. The reflection of the lilies gives the effect of a subdued oil painting.

LINE

CALLA LILIES

The rhythmic lines of the simple and serene Calla lily, so picturesquely cool and velvety, have been arranged in such a way that irregular balance is instinctively apparent. The long stems of the lilies on the left, anchored by means of greening pins to a heavy fruit or vegetable in a crystal bowl, extend out beyond the lilies on the right and provide the needed balance, as well as the sweep of line which makes this illustration so striking.

BRASSAIA RHYTHM

The unique flowers of the Brassaia are arranged in a radiating pattern and silhouetted against a plain, dark-panelled background. The Brassaia, a species of rubber plant, appears in Honolulu gardens as a decorative accent—where its spreading blossoms, like umbrella ribs, reach out in huge sprays of colorful brilliance. Crimson-red torch ginger heads, with their glistening satin petals, add a vivid and congruous touch to this tropical design.

17

RICHNESS AND RHYTHM

Against a woven and gilded Chinese tray, the twisting spray of the Ceylon Morning Glory seed pods, called "Wood Roses," form a delicate, restrained, rhythmic design. The pods, tan and rich brown in color, have been placed in an upside-down, iron Chinese lantern to accentuate the Oriental feeling.

19

HARMONY

Plumeria branches repeat the graceful curve of the bannisters and stairs in a rhythmic, sweeping design. Here, the effect becomes as apparent to the eye as would musical thirds to the ear. The fragrant clusters of plumeria flowers—in pinks and yellows and whites—are seen in many gardens in Hawaii and the Philippines. The flowers are popular in leis (garlands) to express welcome to friends on arrival and bon voyage on their departure.

21

Photo: Werner Stoy

22

AFRICAN TULIP

The magnificent, vivid, scarlet flowers of the African Tulip tree contrast brilliantly both in color and shape with the cinnamon-brown, compactly-clustered, curving buds and the erect sword-shaped seed pods. Here, African Tulip blossoms have been arranged in a woven lauhala (Pandanus) container. The woody texture of the Pandanus, its elegant curves and lines and its neutral color give balance to a design featuring splashing color.

LINE

TRANQUILITY

A modern adaptation of water lilies suggests enchanting beauty and stillness . . . a peaceful brook and its shallows of reeds . . . a placid pool in the early morning and the late evening.

Photo: Werner Stoy

WILD PINEAPPLE FLOWERS

Wild pineapple is rare in Hawaii, where careful cultivation has created a modern industry, but the brilliant flowers of this lovely plant have enormous decorative, as well as nutritive, possibilities. Here, their coral pink and gray-green make an arresting table decoration.

Photo: Werner Stoy

PLUMERIA BLOSSOMS IN A BANANA SHEATH

A peeled, rosy-pink banana sheath taken from the trunk of the growing plant, is used as a container. It is weighted with a solid section of the banana plant into which, as a base, the clusters of cream-colored plumeria flowers are fastened with greening pins. Plumeria leaves in stylized arrangement give rhythmic balance and a bold, original touch. The cream-colored pottery birds, with crimson beaks and combs, repeat and emphasize the illusive colors of nature.

28

Photo: Werner Stoy

DETAIL

The whole leaf of the coconut tree, with its rich yellow stem, is used to cover a tall pedestal. The ribs of the leaf are fitted together in lattice-like pattern to give a decorative effect. This idea has been used in different ways—with a plate glass circular top to hold the large Philodendron leaves or leis (garlands of flowers) draped over the side. Other materials which could be used in place of the coconut leaf to cover the pedestal are stems of the papyrus or tulle grass.

31

BAMBOO AND PLUMERIA

An enchanting pattern in yellow. The plumeria flowers, bamboo, candlesticks and brass container are all variations from the softer glow of the yellow prism. The strong perpendiculars of the arrangement give vitality to the delicate masses, brush-like shadows, and flexible lines.

32

33

CONTRAST WITH TEXTURE

Weeds may be used in the contrast of colors and textures as a medium of expression. Here, rough wild Dock, a riot of tans and rich browns, is the foil for smooth and stylish Iris leaves.

Peter Nyholm

CONTRAST—AND CONGRUITY

Brilliant red Heliconia . . . interesting shapes of the dark brown, circular Enterolobium Cyclocarpum (elephant ear) . . . the texture of mats woven from green coconut fronds—all are vastly different in shape, texture, and color, yet all contribute to the unity and simple elegance of this incidental table arrangement. The seed-pods of the Enterolobium Cyclocarpum have been pinned into a fantastic rose, which acts as a foil to the upright Heliconia stalks.

Photo: Werner Stoy

STUDY IN ROSES AND RHUBARB

Here is a colorful vegetable converted to an unusual and vivid decoration. Pink rambler roses are combined with rhubarb curls, pink rhubarb stems and young rhubarb leaves—all pinned securely on a solid piece of cabbage and laid on a copper tray. Rhubarb curls are made by chilling thin, intensely pink slices in cold water until they curl.

Peter Nyholm

39

ANTHURIUM AND CHINESE CABBAGE

In a composition rhythmic as a native song, Anthurium flowers and leaves bend in studied grace above the pale green frills of Chinese cabbage. The same delicate green is repeated in the table linen, and lacquer luncheon plates emphasize the deep green of the Anthurium leaves.

Photo: Courtesy ''Vogue,'' Condé Nast Publications

Peter Nyholm

ORIENTAL SIMPLICITY

What could be more lovely than the California oak trees with the soft, lacy, gray-green moss dripping from the lichen-covered branches! A wintry composition may be effected with the branches trimmed to balanced proportions and dusted with metallic silver.

ALLUM CETA AND DANCUS CAROTA

Or, to put it more simply—the onion and the carrot! The joy of a surprise is achieved by a rich color contrast between the soft, sea-green of onion stalks, with their dainty pom-pom blossoms, and the orange-yellow chrysanthemums, cut and curled from ordinary carrots.

LOTUS IN A RUSH BASKET

Li Po wrote of ivory Lotus amid the jade green rushes—but he never dreamed of cutting and binding the latter into a basket of superlative beauty. In such a basket of wild reed, or tulle grass, the deep greens eventually change into soft tans and browns with the passage of time. The fragile lace of Avocado blossoms unites the Lotus flowers and their furled leaves with the wide opening of the container. Here West meets East, and utilizes the gifts of both.

MAGNOLIA

The graceful elegance of a Chinese dish is a fitting receptacle for the creamy-white, wax-like freshness of Magnolia blooms. Their dazzling beauty, enhanced by seal-brown leaves from the same tree, create a moderate contrast with the bareness of a weathered branch.

Photo: Werner Stoy

DREAM-LIKE

So simple, so tranquil, yet so eloquent in their message of peace, these water lilies express real beauty and grace and rhythm. To study them is to know the harmony of Nature. The two groupings of water lilies are set apart, the stems of each group curving towards each other, and the unusually pleasing balance is effected by velvety Tahitian spinach leaves on the left and two graceful birds compliment-ing the right. The colorful, stately bamboo provides the background while its soft shadows play through the window to add to the peaceful, dream-like qualities of this arrangement.

Photo: Werner Stoy

BAMBOO

This arrangement of bamboo, used as part of a wedding decoration in an Island home, was placed in heavy jars without water. The cut, open tops of the bamboo were punctured from joint to joint and filled with water—sufficient to enable the bamboo to last several months and to continue to send out green, graceful branches. Nothing in Nature approaches the bamboo in usefulness and beauty. For decorative purposes, it gives strength and delicacy—its leaves and slender twigs throw interesting shadow patterns on backgrounds. Chinese philosophers, poets and painters have attached deep meaning and subtle symbolism to the bamboo—from its strong roots to its slender, brush-stroked leaves.

Photo: Werner Stoy

AMARYLLIS

A backyard garden in Spring or Summer contributes the material for this robust, yet essentially simple, arrangement. Here the large Amaryllis flowers predominate in a bright-colored and delightful design which will brighten the living room or study.

55

FOLIAGE IS IMPORTANT

A simple but pleasant combination of Regal lilies and wild Sumac. In obtaining interesting effects with simple arrangements, foliage can be an important aid. Brilliant marigolds, dahlias, peonies and sweet peas can be made into a glorious design by combining them with strongly textured foliage.

Peter Nyholm

A MONOCHROME

A wheat-sheaf from New England in Hawaiian style becomes a holiday table decoration. Arranged on a copper tray and loosely bound with curling Pandanus leaves, the sheaths of grain express harmony and fulfillment. Wheat, symbolic of the "Staff of Life," may be used with fruits or vegetables to create an arrangement highlighting the festive spirit. The rich beauty of the wheat and corn fields of America are an inspiration to the fashioning of such designs—accented with Iris leaves or corn husks or Pandanus.

Peter Nyholm

A GIFT OF WELCOME

A striking arrangement of Heliconia stalks and blossoms—some in their original state and some created from the imagination. Ribs of the coconut leaf form the perpendicular lines of the basket while other coconut fronds are tied around the basket in pert bows. The flower at the base of the stalks is pure fantasy—having been fashioned from sections cut from the Heliconia sheath and pinned together. The symmetry of the table-top, the basket, and the composition of Heliconia are complimentary, each to the other.

62

CAMELLIAS AND CAT-TAILS

Wind-blown Cat-tails of the reed-like marsh plants, with their dense brown spikes, used with the artistic brown pressed sawdust logs, give architectural departure from any set standards or rules. Here they are combined with the aristocratic flowers and foliage of the Camellia. This arrangement was made in Sacramento, California.

GIFT OF GARDENIAS

This is a refreshing display of a new and distinctive Gardenia, developed by Mr. A. Lewis, Jr., for whom it is named. The Gardenias, spilling informally from a Mexican basket, are brought into relief by using graceful ti leaves in a stylized bow and turned-up ends.

LAND AND SEA

The Birdnest Fern (Ekaha) is from the mountains; the coral from the sea. The long, smooth, leathery leaf of the Ekaha, which perches nest-like in the forest trees and is called "Maui's Paddle" by the Hawaiians, is dark green with shiny black mid-rib. The leaves suggest the mountains; the coral personifies the colorful bed of the sea.

WHERE THE TRADE WINDS BLOW

Fields of sugar cane with their silvery plumes, and the iridescent, jointed cane stalks predominate in this design of contrasting masses. The predominance of the arrangement is due in no small measure to the tropic background of young banana leaves, so interesting in themselves in perfection of line and contour. When the gray cane tassels are sprinkled with silver dust, they make a beautiful festive arrangement—for Christmas or for the New Year.

21

Photo: Werner Stoy

TROPICAL BIZARRE

The stunning leaves of the Traveler's Palm, an ornamental plant which forms the backgrounds of many Hawaiian gardens, is held in a Philippine mahogany container. A member of the banana family, the Traveler's Palm spreads its leaves in the shape of a fan; its flowers are made up of spathes in zig-zag fashion; its effect on observers is dramatic. Shadows, shapes, curves and lines—bizarre blossoms—wind-blown, satiny leaves of many shades—all of these adjectives only partly convey the tropical essence suggested by the Traveler's Palm.

71

PUOLO (A BUNDLE—A GIFT)

Following Hawaiian tradition, the pliant ti-leaves tie up a gift of fruit and wreath it with a fragrant lei of friendship.

73

BIRDS IN FLIGHT

Like birds poised in flight, the glistening white flowers of the Traveler's Palm are dramatically "stopped in action" while springing from their silvery-purple sheaths. A grouping of Pedelanthus leaves anchors the stems of the Traveler's Palm and serves to conceal the spiked holder.

75

THE WHIMSICAL AND IMAGINATIVE

The amusing, bird-like sheaths of the Heliconia flowers preen themselves with delight amid the Iris leaves and their reflections in the plate-glass pool. The jointed bamboo legs of the birds are anchored in sections of banana stalk. Heliconia birds have been used many times as graceful and imaginative table decorations. Their brilliant red beaks and wing-tips, shading into white, create a lively and whimsical motif accented by the subtle background of jade-green Iris leaves.

76

Photo: Werner Stoy

HONEYSUCKLE GARLAND

From time immemorial, leis (garlands) of flowers have symbolized honor and friendship in the Islands. These Honeysuckle flowers were gathered by the wayside in New Jersey and woven into a Hawaiian lei. The soft, creamy yellow blossoms—light, airy, quivering like wings—are threaded through the stems into a lush, fragrant garland. The garland has been doubled and accented with leaves from the Honeysuckle vine itself, thrown informally over a brass bowl and its wooden base. It is not a mere decoration; it is a symbol of friendship and spilled sunshine.

Photo: Courtesy "House & Garden," Condé Nast Publications

Peter Nyholm

HAWAII

"Born was the island
It budded, it leafed
The island blossomed on the tip,
It was green.
T'was Hawaii."

"Ua hanau ka moku
A kupu, a lau, a ao, a muo,
Ka moku iluna,
O Hawaii."

Fornander's Collection, Volume VI, Page 363.